Dear Gameplayer

Your mission is to board the pirate ship *Doom*
and recover the stolen Royal Jewel, which is
hidden in a shield like the one on page five.
Each time you choose which way to go,
you will be told which page to turn to next.
But there are many dangers on board the *Doom*.
Sometimes you can avoid them by finding your way
through a maze, or by looking for something hidden
in the picture. Often you have to use your wits.
Your sole companion is a fox called Rusty,
who is not always very helpful.

Whatever happens you cannot turn back.

Good luck!

Puzzle Master

First published 1991 by Libraire Gründ, Paris
This edition published 2008 by Walker Books Ltd
87 Vauxhall Walk, London SE11 5HJ

2 4 6 8 10 9 7 5 3 1

Text © 1996 Patrick Burston

Illustrations © 1991 Atelier P. Harchy

The right of Patrick Burston and Atelier P. Harchy to be
identified as author and illustrator respectively of this work
has been asserted by them in accordance with the
Copyright, Designs and Patents Act 1988

This book has been typeset in Galliard

Printed in China

British Library Cataloguing in Publication Data
A catalogue record for this book
is available from the British Library.

ISBN 978-1-4063-1776-3

www.walkerbooks.co.uk

PUZZLE MASTER

The Pirates of Doom

Patrick Burston

illustrated by **Atelier P. Harchy**

WALKER BOOKS
AND SUBSIDIARIES
LONDON · BOSTON · SYDNEY · AUCKLAND

The pirate ship *Doom* is about to leave the harbour. There doesn't seem to be anyone about, so now is your chance to get on board. Which way will you go?

If you choose to climb along the rope, turn to page 10. If you decide to go up the gangplank, turn to page 8.

If you go up these
steps, turn to page 14.

You are in the ship's hold,
where the gunpowder is kept.
Five trails of gunpowder have
caught fire, but only one of
them leads to a gunpowder
barrel. Find which one, so
that you can save the ship.
(Trace each trail with
your finger.)

If you go through this door, turn to page 12.

9

You're on deck, but someone's coming. Find a way to set the cannonballs rolling to trip them up.

If you escape up these steps, turn to page 14.

If you go this way, turn to page 16.

If you climb out of the
window, turn to page 20.

If you climb out of the
window, turn to page 20.

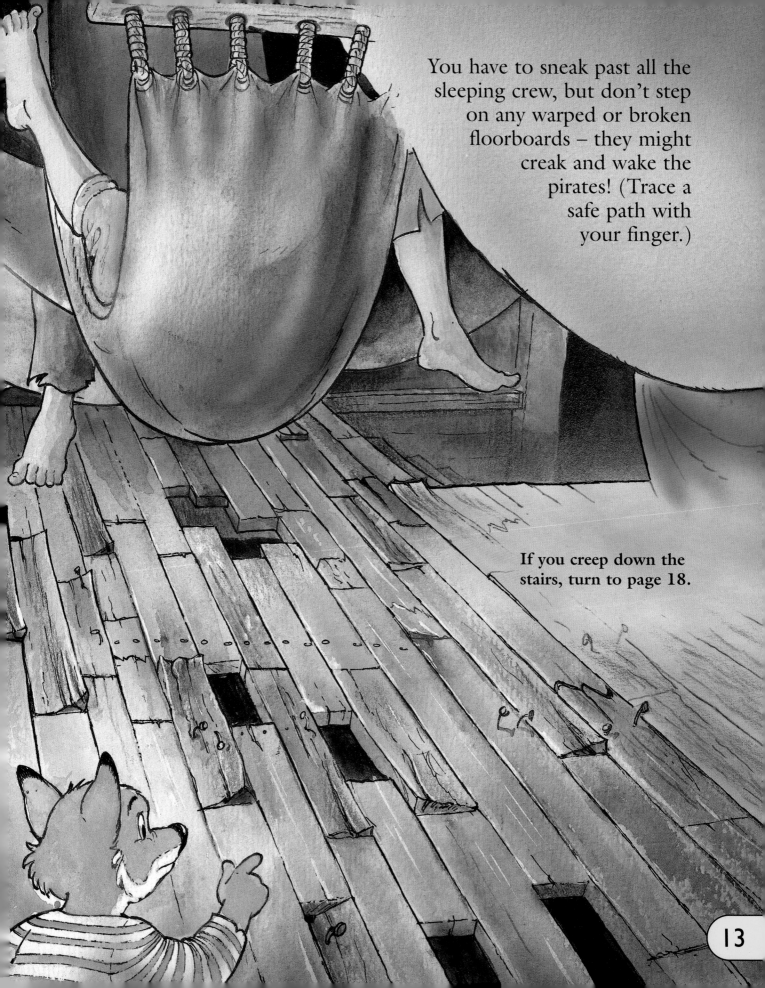

You have to sneak past all the sleeping crew, but don't step on any warped or broken floorboards – they might creak and wake the pirates! (Trace a safe path with your finger.)

If you creep down the stairs, turn to page 18.

The ship's wheel has been
tied fast with a rope and you
are heading for those rocks!
Find something shaped like a
sword to cut the rope, then
steer the ship to safety.

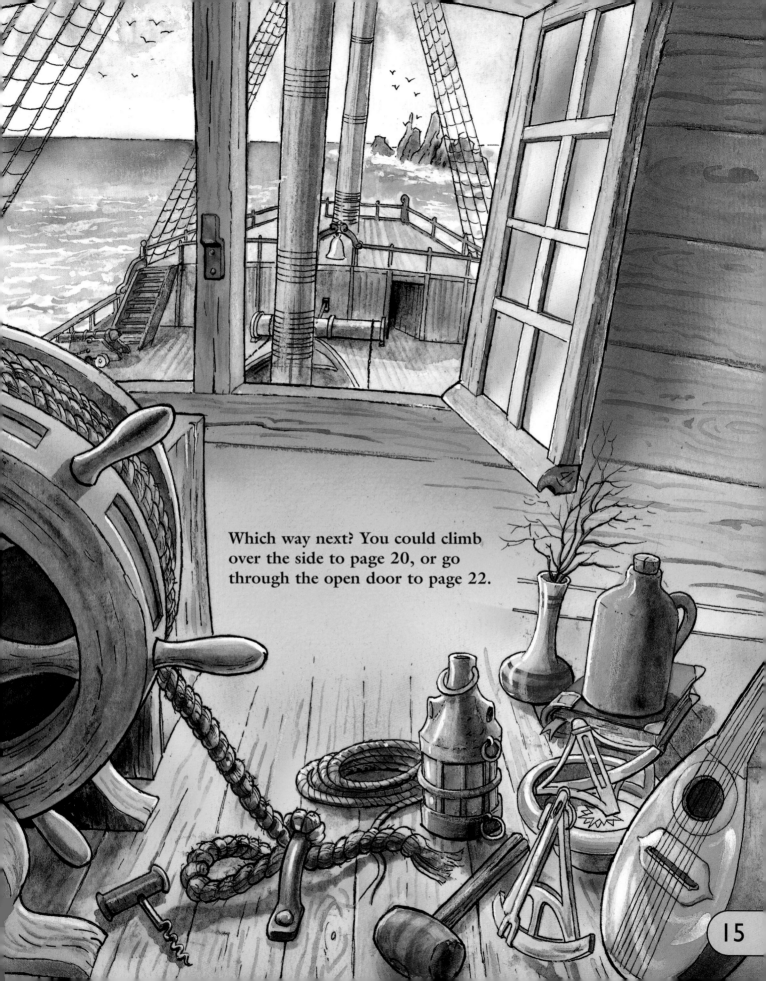

Which way next? You could climb over the side to page 20, or go through the open door to page 22.

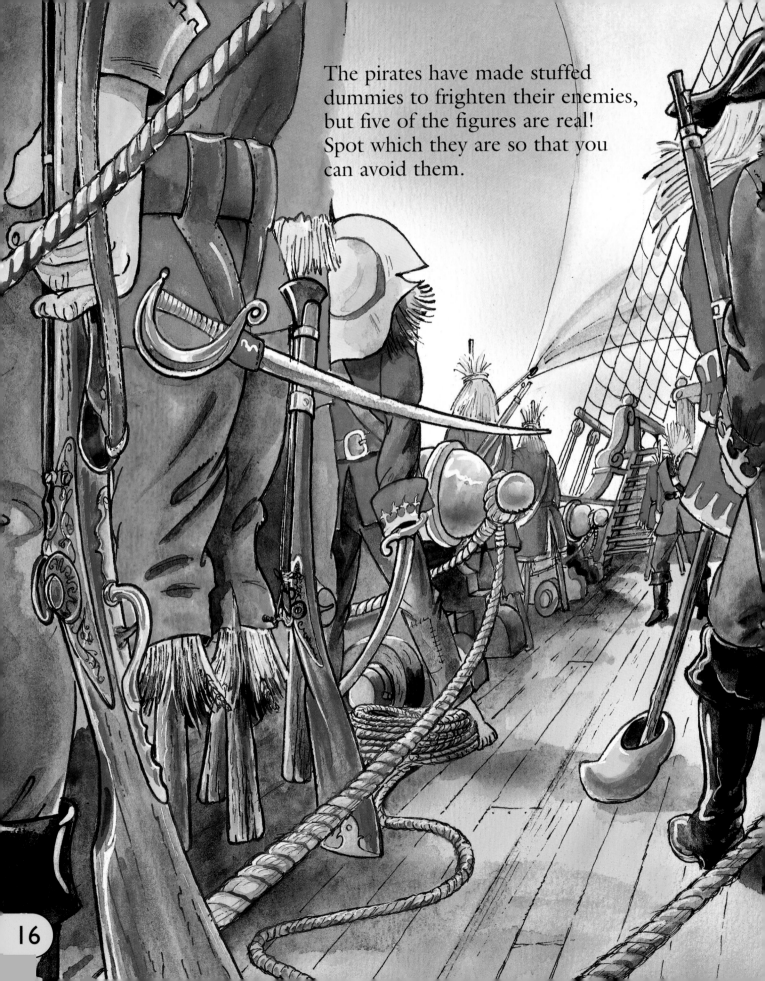

The pirates have made stuffed dummies to frighten their enemies, but five of the figures are real! Spot which they are so that you can avoid them.

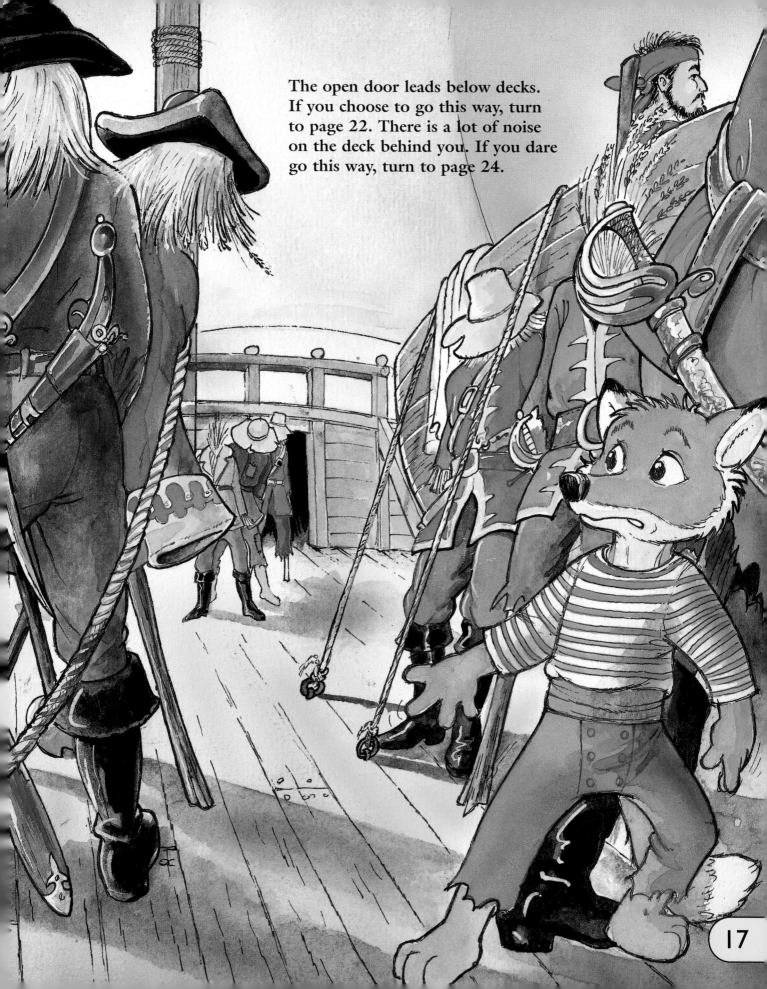

The open door leads below decks. If you choose to go this way, turn to page 22. There is a lot of noise on the deck behind you. If you dare go this way, turn to page 24.

The ship's armoury! Find the five hidden keys so that you can unlock the pirates' weapons and throw them overboard. Then choose which way to go next.

If you go through the door, turn to page 28.

If you choose to go down the steps, turn to page 26.

You've heard of people having to "walk the plank"– well, now it's your turn. To escape you will have to swing on one of those ropes down to one of the two open portholes. But take care! Only one of the ropes is fastened to anything. Find which one.

Turn to page 28.

Turn to page 30.

If you go through this
door, turn to page 32.

You're in the Captain's cabin,
and you can hear him behind
that screen. Find his wooden
leg and throw it out of the
porthole so that he can't
chase you!

22

If you decide to go down these steps, turn to page 30.

23

The *Doom* has been boarded by enemy pirates and you're in the thick of the fighting. Count the pirates. If there are the same number with red headbands as there are with black headbands you can escape.

Did you escape? If so, you can use the ladder to go down that open hatch to page 32, or nip up the mast to page 34.

Turn to page 36.

Turn to page 42.

Horrible serpents are lurking in the depths of the ship. Find a way between them through the shallow water. (Trace a path with your finger.) It's safe to cross the ropes.

In the pirates' treasure chamber a magic doll has conjured up an evil spirit. To cancel the spell find another green doll.

Hurry! Choose which way to go!
Out of the porthole to page 36,
or up those steps to page 38.

The cook has spilled flour all over the galley floor. Now he is asleep in the corner. You must creep past him, without stepping in the flour and leaving footprints. (Trace a path with your finger.) You can climb across the furniture if you need to.

Turn to page 38.

Turn to page 40.

The Captain's table is
spread with a sumptuous
feast. You're hungry,
but before you can
eat you must spot
eight nasty things
hiding among
the food.

Which way now? To climb
the ladder, turn to page 40.
If you think that parrot
is showing you the way,
turn to page 42.

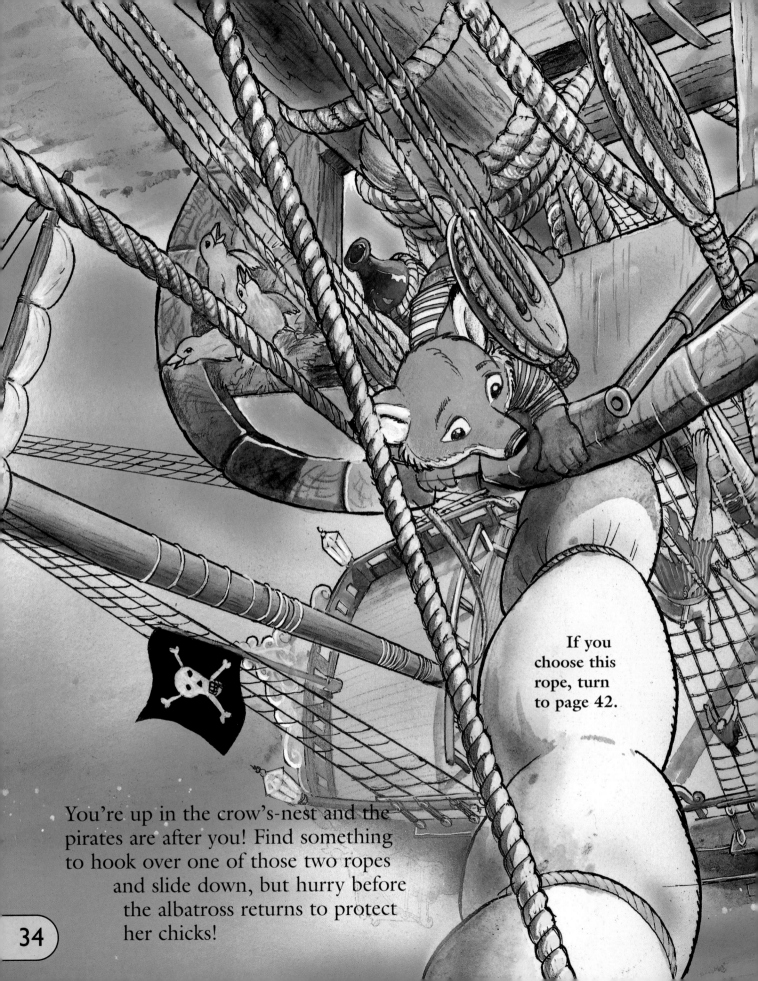

If you choose this rope, turn to page 42.

You're up in the crow's-nest and the pirates are after you! Find something to hook over one of those two ropes and slide down, but hurry before the albatross returns to protect her chicks!

If you choose
this rope, turn
to page 44.

Beware! Sharks! If you stay close to the ship the outline of a dolphin will scare them off. Can you spot it?

You have failed to find the Royal Jewel. Swim back to page 6 so you can try again!

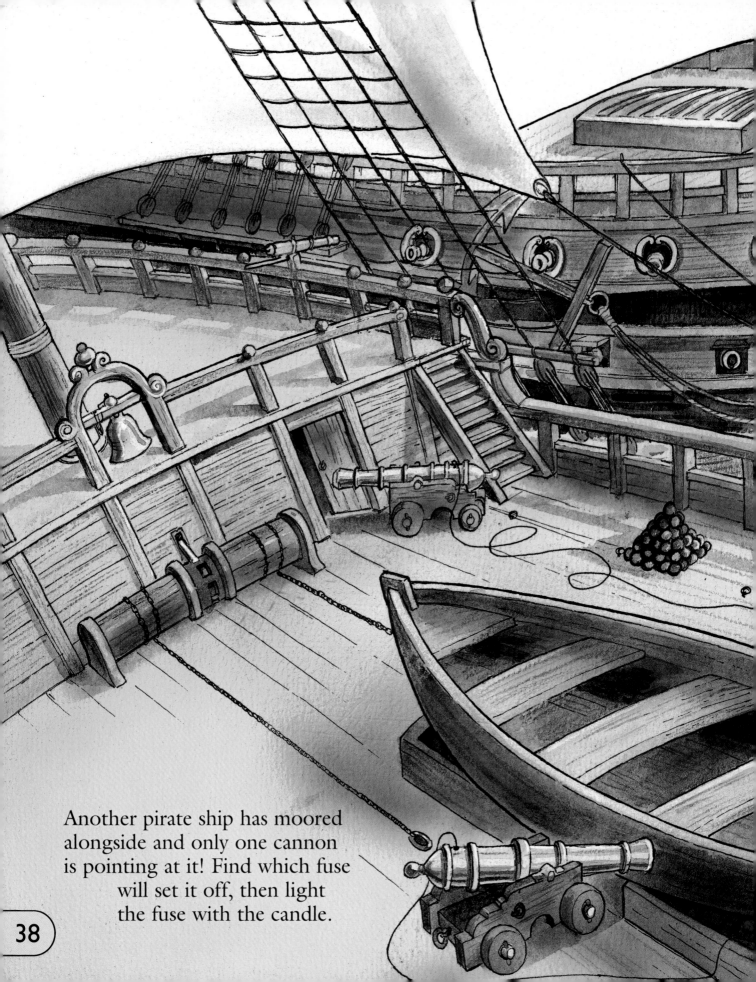

Another pirate ship has moored alongside and only one cannon is pointing at it! Find which fuse will set it off, then light the fuse with the candle.

You still have not found the Royal Jewel, so go back to page 6 and try again.

The flame from that lantern has started a fire. You must alert the pirate without him seeing you. Somewhere near Rusty is your loaded catapult. Find it and wake the pirate by firing at the bell above his head.

You have saved the ship, but must go back to page 6 and start again to find the Royal Jewel.

The parrot has torn three maps in half but only the map Rusty's holding will lead you to hidden treasure. Find the other half and you can claim the reward one day. But for now you must return to page 6 and try again to find the Royal Jewel.

Now's your chance to find the Royal Jewel. Can you remember what it looks like? (You saw it on page 5.) The pirates have all gone ashore to the island, so you and Rusty can sail the ship home.

YOUR QUEST IS ENDED.
WELL DONE!

Answers

10
pull the rope to send the cannonballs rolling in all directions

14
you can use the swordfish on the wall to cut the rope

24
there are equal numbers of pirates with red headbands and black headbands – 15 of each

32
- a caterpillar in the lettuce
- a crab among the pineapples
- a grub in the mangoes
- a red spider on the tomatoes
- a snake among the cucumbers
- a centipede under the napkin
- a tentacle reaching from the jug
- a bee in the honeypot